# cicadas in the belly

Jessicamarie Wermes

BookLeaf Publishing

India | USA | UK

Presentation by *BookLeaf Publishing*

Web: www.bookleafpub.com

E-mail: info@bookleafpub.com

ISBN: 9789360946579

First edition 2024

*to every person i have ever loved and the
cicadas they have birthed from the soil of my
heart.*


*and for Brigid, the goddess of poetry.*

# ACKNOWLEDGEMENT

thank you, ian and meagan, my best friends and favorite muses. without both of you i wouldn't be here today nor would any of my poetry ever have seen a page.

# love.

i wish i could say i love you and mean it
or
i wish i wasn't a girl made of wounds
and my lover
always
the salt
by that i mean
i never love the right person
so my throat becomes a mirror
mimic sentiment
till i am nothing more then façade
you foolishly
fall
in love with
because even now
the word spills from my lips like a slur
and worse of all
i wish i really did love you
i wish i could give you something you deserve
but it seems
wishing
is the only emotion i feel

# the fall.

and i crumbled under the weight of you. nursing wounds from a tongue that only ever savored the ruin of little girls. fluorescent lights have a way of tricking the eye and i believed your illusion because don't all 15 year olds when handed wax wings. promises glittering like fools gold. you called me icarus like the sun refusing to take accountability for its actions. i was always too sensitive. too emotional. and like predator to pray, you found a way to use that against me.

# feral  b i t e , loving  d e v o u r

your teeth graze my skin and i dare you to leave
a  m a r k.  a omen of your flickering existence. a
claim to what will always be just a flesh wound
away from being yours. what i don't tell you is
how i crave your violence,  p h y s i c a l
e v i d e n c e  for all these invisible fingerprints
you leave. a sign of the times, a sign of a crime
but sentiment the sweetest con. your wit  f e r a l
and unrelenting leaves only scars in its place. so
i dare you to bite down, till flesh gives in and
jaw bone breaks. tell me what our blood tastes
like when mixed together.
b i t t e r
s w e e t
swallowing verity till we regurgitate lies.
because when i tell you to  b i t e  me there is no
hesitation in finding my skin to your mouth.
nibbles leaving pink crescent moon silhouettes.
this action too gentle for comfort. to gentle for
the savagery that is you and i.

when i tell you to  b i t e  me,
 i really mean  d e v o u r  me whole.

the man at the game store
remembers our first date,
says he and his coworker
made bets we'd fall in love.

it's been a year since then and we spend the
weekend getting high and licking strawberry
sugar off our fingers. laying in the grass we
pretend to have seen each other more than two
times this year. we take photos in our skirts to
make this worth getting dressed up for. and the
most important conversation we can seem to
have is you explaining marvel movie logic to a
girl who would rather be watching true crime.
we argue on the walk to the store about the heat
and when the guy says he's owed ten dollars
now, i feel the lie constricting my tongue. i've
never known what true love feels like but i know
that cats slowly blink to show affection so i walk
around blinking at your grumpy cat. determined
to get sentiment despite the claws. and isn't that
just like me, wanting love where there is only
pain. still trying regardless of the
outcome.

# the story of the lamp and moth is one of fatal attraction

so

do moths flutter around you like needy
heartbeats
        craving the warmth of you
                aflame by mere touch


        i know the danger in men who radiate light

like i know the burns
that trace my own skin
from kindling sentiment

you wear allure well
        temptation cloaked in the smirk of your lips
secret
        [stolen]
    looks exchanged in crowded rooms
and isn't it poetic how in the palm of your hand
        i become more moth then girl

        a fragile thing
whose fate is to be crumpled
worse yet scorched

by a love you refuse to give
by a man so poignantly
                    luminescent


and like a moth to a flame
    i sacrifice myself just to be close to you

# as many now as we can get

somewhere. in some universe. there is a line of fate connecting me to you. connecting summer camp classrooms to black tie dinners to the first bus ride of freshman year. there is a statistic out there for calculating the chances of us knowing exactly the right person to collide like planets. how we were destined to supernova. and somewhere there is a delicate strand of gold connecting ed sheeran to jealous ex boyfriends to choir auditions. wrapped around matching necklaces and laced fingers, how we always said too much, but never enough. falling apart and falling back together. ten years tangled. connecting high school football to orange and green halloween lights to the undone button on your pants. the yin and yang of us clashing like opposing magnets. always too emotional, too callous. three words. two meanings. and somewhere. some universe. it will always be  us tied together.
me and you.

# and if the poet is at a loss for words

if the red paints her cheeks

and giggles froth from her chapped lips

if her eyes dart from you like a receding tide

and metaphors disappear behind the crescent
moon of her smile

if she bares her palms

small and caught

like a child with a sweet tooth for something

someone

she just can't understand is bad for her

if in your poisoning

the heart on her sleeve turns to cellophane

and her teeth dull from biting back predators
wearing gentlemen's clothing

if you kiss vulgarity into a girl young enough to
be your daughter, reach your fingers in, do you
still expect to find the flame in the back of her
throat

because if the poet is at a loss for words

that is when you have finally broken her

# parasitically tangled

i suppose you think me a masochist
staying long after the pain of us
turned me into a hollow forest
but it was never the torment of your love
that i feared the most
life grows even in death
no
it was the trepidation of living
without the fevered warmth of your fire
without the sharp steel of your ax
without you
to carve your way into me
that kept my roots curled around yours
because who am i without you to define me
and without pain to define love

# tender.

sink your fingers into my
tender tangerine flesh
sweet juices spill past your knuckles
in a effort to dribble on the floor
look how i overflow
just for you
offer up my diaphanous pulp
just for you to call me cellophane
call me rotten fruit
you peel back my layers
and swallow all that makes me desirable
taking for granted the sensual flavors to your
tongue
and  i wonder how any nature can stay soft at
your callous touch
can stay whole in the face of your ruin
clenched fists around blossoms disguised as
wrists
orchards clandestine throats
and we are taught to grow for these men
fructescence molded into that which nurtures
everyone but our very own roots
claiming our beauty for their own
and watch me swell
just for you

just like i'm supposed to
gustatory modality as they pick the ripest fruit
worst yet coarse throats squawk like predatory
crows
say consent tastes like moldering rinds
like bitter juice
because
we are the naked oranges
and they the ravenous mouths

# (love, i mean.)

i'm high and laying in your bed. i recognize
your fingers intertwined with mine, how they are
cold to my hot. yet i stare at the dancing
shadows on your ceiling so sure i'm floating
away from you. so sure this bed is our grave.
you're asleep and i breathe like i have forgotten
how to while you're awake. choking on a tongue
that only ever told you lies. i look for a pulse
with a heart that stopped beating when i was
twelve, muscle memory punishes you for the
sins of a boy who never loved me back. and i'm
sober enough to know it shouldn't feel like this. i
shouldn't feel alone when i'm right next to you.
distance makes us more label than love so i
spend the rest of the night dreaming of ways to
apologize for the wreckage you never knew i
made us.

# the sensational death of a little piggy

and i'd flirt with the flame
just to get high off the burn

    masochistic longing
    leading my feet from
        rain soaked pavement
          into his car
this, the moment
where the audience knows
sad girl
      stupid girl
          dead girl
never feeling
the night sky pressing in
and how the warmth of a

    wolf

is better then standing

         alone

in the cold

# STRANGLED

[ afraid of the venom
inside each other's mouths
we make it a game
to see who can land
the fatal bite first.
who can poke at the
most tender parts
without coming away
black and blue.
love a vulnerable rabbit
and our words
the hungry snake.
we crave the blush
of necrosis.
emotions strangled
by raw throats.
finding it's easier
to draw blood
then nurture the gentle
of a beating heart. ]

# marriage pact lovers were not made for february 14th

getting tangled in the red and pink trap that is
valentine's day, you stare out from where you
left me on this perch. intertwine your fingers
with another and label me a second choice. your
top shelf back up if this boy too, disastrously
unravels you. and how flattered i should be at
this game of coy lovers and gold bands forged
out of necessity. out of fear of being lonely.

 and i know the rotting i love yous caught in
your throat are saved just for me. make me a
special kind of secret, a fall back again love. but
they sound so pretty verbalized to another i can't
help but want it's caressing touch. can't help but
envy the soft silk on display.

and perhaps i should be more grateful, ten years
my name has fallen from your lips, etched on
your skin. i realize for some this sticky glazed
holiday is a lonely affair, that is void of platonic
lovers tangled in promises.

but i only feel like a lie. a false façade.
marionetted devotee by circumstance.

we are a house made out of paper-mâché hearts
with a foundation laid in longing, fear a much
stronger motivator than love. because out of fear
we grasp at things less than hoping to make
them whole, hoping to make them what they are
not and never will be.

i can't presume to know how this shakespearean
sonnet will end but i know i'm not fine china for
your shelf. counting fourteen days and fourteen
ways i was more yours then he and that's the
worst of it. i always will be.

so as you show off your jeweled lover just
remember who you will come home to. because
in the end, valentine's day only celebrates the
ever waning emotions of affection. never the
fine line of love and hate that you will live with
day to day.

# delusions from a starving girl:

i claw at the scraps of you
my heart aching with hunger
poetry rests in the belly
and i try to vomit it to paper
only to become bulimic with want
you let me lick the electricity
off of an accidental touch
my fingers stained
the color of your irises
from picking at the fruit of your attention
devouring your sugar coated words
i regurgitate back what's agreeable
and by that i mean
you feed me just enough of your high
to keep this starving girl coming back
for more

  and i'll stuff my face with the sweetest
tasting delusion
     if it means i get to
feel love in my belly.

# soiled

like black ink
staining white lace
your just too soft
for the bruise
that blooms on your skin
hungry mouths
mark you like a hunted
wounded
thing
devoured and spit back out
like tarnished creamware tea sets
and yellowing pearls
yanked off delicate necks
he carelessly paws
with desire
at breakable things
because
i know what
a chip
in your porcelain
feels like
and how quickly it can become
a crack

# does my name taste as sweet in your mouth as it sounds falling from your lips

vending machine, root beer bottles and syrup colored eyes. two dollars buys me your admiration so i leave caution in my wallet, next to the cupcakes receipt. wondering if your hands are shaking too i decide it's best not to know. to remember you gentle. like ribbons in hair or the swish of my skirt you watch as i walk away. your voice, my name. you have a way of bending my will, giving into gravity. i don't think twice when you open your arms for me, this something i so naturally give i worry about the puzzle piece warp when we part. but hands find shoulder blades, your beard to the crook of my neck. count the seconds, grip me tighter. i feel you crave me then the way i ache for your tenderness. your flush cheeks and body heat. two humans supernova and when the absence of you pricks my flesh, nothing will have changed. life goes on. this moment meaning everything and yet nothing at all.

# dinner.

carving myself into this man
i lay
head on his chest
leg hooked around his
spooning intimacy onto my tongue
like the salt of his skin
    this
the way i love
gorging myself
on the sentiment of others

and he bites back
mouthfuls of this soft flesh
savoring the pain
pink petals bloom to the skin
yellow and wilt with age
    this
the way he satiates
devouring
the gentle served to him

# like slicing secrets

i could peel my skin like an orange
or an apple
and still not be rid of his touch
still not be rid of the carve
nor the bruise of porcelain tile
this flesh now as rotten
as the soul who imprinted it
bone marrow poisoned
by a boy who's greed
seeped through his wandering hands
and like slicing secrets from a corpse
i swallow my own tongue
choke on my voice
that froths the sickly
sweetness of a silent victim
girl turned bruised peach
i was just fruit in a bowl
ripe for the taking

# himeros eat my heart out

sipping attention out of the palm of your hand, i
get drunk off the allure you. turning me into a
mess of flush cheeks and girlish giggles, i can't
remember when you turned into sin. into secret
indulgence. your liquor eyes linger, make an
addict out of a careful creature. and now i can't
get the taste of your name off my tongue, you
the sugar hidden underneath. our words hang
heavy and sweet. like molasses licked off lips.
your touch cannibalistic and i starved of
affection give into the gluttony of you. this
lustful bloat of the heart poisoning me till all i
become is love sick.

# of salt and wounds

you never savored the ruining
you were more of a disastrous man
watching as your own tears
reddened my wounds
this crucifixion
disguised as martyrdom
burning the back of my throat
all the words never said
and
slow was the poisoning
cyanotic love
crumbling charade
iodized tenderness
i never noticed
the way your hands
curled around
left bruises on
and tangled in
till nothing of me
wasn't touched by you

# i want to sip wine with you

i want to sip wine with you
talk of nostalgia
spilling cherry blood
i want to cradle your collarbone
and kiss the stubble of your jaw
whisper my hurt into the darkness
while you curl your arms around my waist
and promise to never let go
i need you to promise
or else
i fear i'll wither
turning to dust in the wind
being condemned to float

and so we get drunk cus we can't face ourselves
only i'm in the mirror of your eyes
our monsters have each other's faces
and i'm content in kissing them away
but you are more lyric than poem
and we are soulmates but not of the lover kind
so i cry into the fabric that smells like you
you go stoic but look at me eyes filled with an
ocean
even at the bottom of a bottle

i know i'm the only one you'll ever look at like
that
i'm the only fire you'll bother putting out
so i waver between your sharp tongue and
toxicity
the way a drug addict wavers between the high
and the crash
heaven and hell

i want to chip away your marble
to touch the silk underneath
without losing your opulence
but to do so would crack our very foundation
crumble years of tongue in cheek façade
rot our vines we have so carefully intertwined
and darling i know better then to take a wrecking
ball
to dynasties just to marvel at the damage

so we sit with the music
communicate with each rise and fall of our chest
i let this moment consume me
let you consume me
rose color
and
rose quartz
i hold on to the good
pretend the bad, a mirage

and this isn't to say i don't get cut by your
shards
draped elegantly in trauma
i do
but you know i too rub salt in your wounds
sadistical merriment at my power
to make you
    b u r n

and darling
this is why i stay
in war torn bedrooms
why i sip wine with you
in infinite time loops
forever repeating
because we have always been and always will be
an elegant wreckage